LISTEN   BRIEF FIFTH EDITION

LISTEN

BRIEF FIFTH EDITION

JOSEPH KERMAN
University of California, Berkeley

GARY TOMLINSON
University of Pennsylvania

with
VIVIAN KERMAN

BEDFORD/ST. MARTIN'S
Boston ◆ New York

For Bedford/St. Martin's

Developmental Editor: Maura Shea
Senior Production Editor: Karen S. Baart
Senior Production Supervisor: Dennis Conroy
Marketing Manager: Jenna Bookin Barry
Editorial Assistant: Anne Noyes
Production Assistants: Michaela Dodd, Kristen Merrill
Copyeditor: Clia M. Goodwin
Text Design: Malcolm Grear Designers; revised by Wanda Kossak
Cover Design: Donna Lee Dennison
Cover Art: Dominique Guillemard, *La Phalange.* Courtesy of Galerie Arpé, Cannes, France
Composition and Layout: DeNee Reiton Skipper
Music Composition: A-R Editions, Inc.
Printing and Binding: R.R. Donnelley & Sons Company

President: Joan E. Feinberg
Editorial Director: Denise B. Wydra
Editor in Chief: Karen S. Henry
Director of Marketing: Karen Melton
Director of Editing, Design, and Production: Marcia Cohen
Managing Editor: Elizabeth M. Schaaf

Library of Congress Control Number: 2003101702

Manufactured in the United States of America.

8   7   6   5
f   e   d   c

For information, write: Bedford/St. Martin's, 75 Arlington Street, Boston, MA 02116
(617-399-4000)

ISBN: 0–312–40115–9 (paperback)
      0–312–41123–5 (hardcover)

Acknowledgments

Preface
To the Instructor

imes have changed in the nearly thirty years since *Listen* first appeared, and with them the book has changed substantially. Instructors familiar with previous editions of this textbook will observe three main changes in *Listen*, Brief Fifth Edition. The first is a return, in a simpler version, of the "Overture" idea used in earlier editions. Heard on the CD-ROM packaged with the book, our Study Guide, the March to the Scaffold from Berlioz's *Fantastic* Symphony can give students an immediate listening experience, which is also a learning experience, to light up day one in any music course. We talk about this a little more below.

Next, the short listening exercises in Unit I (Fundamentals) have been much expanded, and music provided for them on the CD-ROM. There are a dozen short excerpts illustrating rhythm, melody, texture, and so on, plus the redoubtable *Young Person's Guide to the Orchestra* by Benjamin Britten. We show students how to listen to this work as an informal summary of fundamentals at the end of Unit I.

A third change is in the sections on non-Western music. Some have been dropped and others grouped together after the book's main units, under the name *Global Perspectives*. This grouping has been done programmatically, yielding more substantial teaching elements, we believe, as well as fewer interruptions to the basic text.

In addition, responding to many thoughtful suggestions from readers, we have once again worked to improve the selection of music for the CD sets, our basic teaching materials. Some of the changes are significant: See plainchant, the symphony, and music of the late twentieth century. The coverage of popular music has been expanded, though to do it full justice here with recorded examples was not feasible.

What has not changed is our basic coverage, organization, treatment, and style, which have proved so solid over many editions. For new users, we draw attention to the following strong features that we believe set *Listen* apart:

Overture Most instructors work out a special introductory session to break the ice and interest students in the subject matter of their course. The Overture to this book is a specific suggestion for such an ice-breaker—students listen to a short, rousing piece, the March to the Scaffold from Berlioz's *Fantastic* Symphony, with a short commentary that will give them a taste of what the semester will be like. (The Overture also provides an easy introduction to the Listening Charts that are so important to the book.) At this stage the emphasis is on direct impressions rather than on terminology, but some technical terms are introduced in passing, terms that will be presented formally in Unit I.

❡ *Overall organization*   The book's coverage is simple and clear, and evident at once from the listing of "Contents in Brief," on page xix. (This may seem like an elementary, obvious thing, but in our judgment not a few texts give first impressions that are muddled and forbidding.) After "Fundamentals," the historical scheme goes from "Early Music"—in effect, everything before Bach and Handel, when the standard repertory begins—to the three great periods of Western classical music: the eighteenth, nineteenth, and twentieth centuries. Each century is treated as a unit—Unit III, Unit IV, and Unit V—containing several chapters.

❡ *Flexible coverage*   Coverage—that perpetual (and probably insoluble) problem for instructors, and for textbook writers also! How much time or space does one devote to music of the so-called common-practice period, and how much to Early Music and music of the twentieth century? How much to popular music? Music from beyond Europe and America?

The main emphasis of *Listen* is on the common-practice repertory, basically for reasons of time. Only so much can be accomplished in a semester course, and most instructors will agree that students learn more from exposure to a limited amount of material in some depth than from overambitious surveys. Probably all agree that beginning courses in music should introduce students to the good music they will most likely hear in later life.

By the end of many a semester, the final pages of books like this one tend be sacrificed on account of time constraints. For those who would rather save time at the beginning, Unit II, "Early Music: An Overview," has been made *strictly optional* in the book's sequence. Nothing later in the book depends on having studied it, so if your course plan begins with Unit III, "The Eighteenth Century," no one will need to skip back for explanations of continuo texture, recitative, fugue, and so on.

And for those who prefer to use some selections of early music without teaching the entire unit, the fairly modest amount of prose in Unit II should prove manageable as a general orientation for the music chosen.

❡ *Non-Western music*   The Global Perspectives segments are positioned so as to elaborate the European and American topics discussed around them. Three of them come at the ends of the Early Music chapters; they take up sacred chant (at the end of the Middle Ages chapter), European colonialism (Renaissance), and ostinato techniques (early Baroque). Two more, on African drumming and on global pop, come in the last chapter, "Jazz and Beyond." The remaining two segments come at the ends of the eighteenth- and nineteenth-century units of the book and treat, respectively, complexities of form in instrumental music and musical drama. We believe we have tailored these materials so that they can broaden in a meaningful way the coverage of *Listen*, but we certainly do not offer them as a token survey of world musics. If they are a token of anything, it is the authors' belief that music-making worldwide shows certain common, deep tendencies in which the European classical tradition has shared.

❡ *Cultural background*   The Baroque and Classical eras and the nineteenth and twentieth centuries are introduced by what we call "Prelude" chapters. These summarize some features of the culture of the times, in particular those that can be seen to affect music. (Generously captioned color illustrations for these chapters, and others, are an original *Listen* specialty that has now become a standard textbook feature.) The Prelude chapters also contain concise accounts of the musical styles of the eras, so that these chapters furnish background of two kinds—cultural and stylistic—for listening to specific pieces of music in the chapters that follow.

❧ *Recordings* The main compositions studied in *Listen* are available in multiple recordings, and much time and effort has gone into searching for what seem to us the best ones. (The search becomes increasingly difficult as licensing rights are denied by more and more record companies.) It is gratifying to learn from market research that many users consider our choices superior. We hope that instructors and students will get the same charge out of our selections that we do, and it's our further fond hope that students may keep these recordings and keep listening to them in future years.

Seventy-seven of the selections discussed in the text appear on the accompanying 6-CD set. The 3-CD set contains thirty-three selections. (To allow for the maximum use of disc space, a few selections in the CD sets appear out of order: that is, not in the sequence of their appearance in the book. The Global Perspectives tracks have all been put at the ends of the CDs.) An icon tells the listener *which number* CD to select from the sets (this is the numeral inside the circle) and then *which track* to play (the numeral below it). The Study Guide CD-ROM has its own icon with track numbers marked below it.

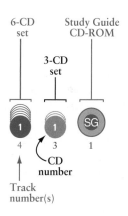

❧ *Design* Obviously this book is attractive to look at (an early version of it won a design award). But the real point of a good design is to make it easy to find your way around in a book and make the book inviting to use. If the temptation to cram more and more into a text is not resisted, the text will be cluttered and confused and will itself be resisted by its targeted readership.

In particular, we think the *Listen* format for Listening Charts is superior. The charts all fit onto one page, visible at a glance, with concise descriptions and identifications. Off at the side, brief music tags can easily be consulted by those who read music—and just as easily ignored by those who don't. As to the timings, in selections divided into several CD tracks, the timings to the *left* of the vertical rule give the time elapsed from the start of the previous track, while those to the *right* of the rule give the total time from the start of the piece.

Standardized biography boxes segregate material on the lives of the major composers from discussions of their music—again, making the book easier to read and easier to work from. The boxes all include portraits, concise lists of works that can serve for study or reference, and, under the heading "Encore," suggestions for further listening.

And we think we have introduced some new elements in an uncluttered way: a certain number of maps throughout the text, and quick references to resources on the Web site. (See under "Supplements Package" for a complete description of the Web site.) We have expanded the time lines to show historical events and movements as well as individuals.

❧ *Appendix* "Further Listening, Suggested Readings, and Recommended Web Sites" provides students with recommendations for audio, print, and online materials for further study and (we hope, once again) reference for a lifetime of engagement with music. Suggestions for further listening go beyond the Encore recommendations given in the composer biographies and extend to world music and jazz. The readings are mostly standard reference works, with a few of the authors' personal favorites included. Finally, "Recommended Web Sites" gives URLs of useful sites related to the composers and non-Western cultures covered in the text as well as some excellent general music sites containing a broad range of relevant topical information. Brief annotations make it easy to scan the list and quickly find the Web resource needed. These Web addresses also appear in the "Links" section of the companion Web site (bedfordstmartins.com/listen) where students and instructors alike can find valuable learning and teaching aids.

Supplements Package

Recognizing how much the teaching and learning experience of this course may be enhanced through a mixture of media, we have updated and expanded the supplements for the Brief Fifth Edition as follows:

❧ The **Study Guide CD-ROM** is entirely new and bound into each copy of the book. It provides two valuable, essential resources. First, it contains the thirteen audio recordings (listed below) that correspond to the new listening exercises in Unit I, including Benjamin Britten's *Young Person's Guide to the Orchestra*. Second, it presents all of the book's Listening Charts in a newly enhanced interactive format. These multimedia charts encourage the listener to delve more deeply into major works through guided multiple listenings.

1–3	Berlioz, *Fantastic* Symphony, IV, March to the Scaffold
4	Schubert, from Symphony No. 8 ("Unfinished"), I
5	Joplin, "Maple Leaf Rag"
6	Rachmaninov, from *Rhapsody on a Theme by Paganini*
7	Gershwin, "Who Cares?"
8	Beethoven, "Joy Theme" from Symphony No. 9, IV
9	Stravinsky, from *Symphony of Psalms,* II
10	Schubert, Moment Musical No. 3
11	Beethoven, from Piano Concerto No. 5 ("Emperor")
12	Mahler, from Symphony No. 1, III
13	Chaikovsky, from *The Nutcracker Suite:* Dance of the Sugar-Plum Fairy
14–16	Beethoven, Symphony No. 5, III
17–22	Britten, *The Young Person's Guide to the Orchestra*

❧ The **companion Web site *Listen Online*** at bedfordstmartins.com/listen is now integrated with the book (references throughout the text direct students to related content on the Web site) and newly expanded to include listening and content quizzes for every chapter, demos (real, not synthesized) and photographs of instruments of the orchestra, interactive Listening Charts, annotated research links organized by chapter, vocabulary flashcards, a hyperlinked glossary, and other instructor and student resources. (See illustration on facing page.)

❧ The *Instructor's Resource Manual* (prepared by Mark Harbold) offers Chapter Outlines, Important Terms, Teaching Objectives, and Lecture Suggestions for each chapter, as well as Class Discussion Ideas, Lecture-Demonstration Ideas, Listening Ideas, and hundreds of Further Listening Examples going beyond the textbook chapters. A Multimedia Resources section gives many suggestions for video, DVD, and software enhancements, additional Listening Charts, and much more.

Introduction
To the Student

The Virgin Megastore in San Francisco is a grand space with walls nearly as high as the floor is wide. A dozen monitors promoting videos of the newest singles look down on bins of CDs divided up between the many kinds of popular music. Near a tall window looking out onto the street, handsome escalators lead up to the second floor, the place for World Music, Jazz, and—behind soundproof glass doors—Classical. On the third floor, DVDs, Software, and Customer Service.

A Rip van Winkle waking up after a fifty-year sleep in the redwood groves would be amazed at the variety of music available, and even more amazed that all the different kinds could be played, one right after another, on an apparatus called a CD player costing the equivalent of a 1950s ten-spot. Multiplicity and instant availability are twin attributes of today's culture. Music megastores exist to feed that culture. Bookstores are an older example of the same phenomenon, with their multiple shelves for Fiction, Business, Cooking—and even Music. A newer example is the Internet.

And in the spirit of multiplicity, our idea in this book is to bring classical music out from behind those soundproof glass doors so that it can live harmoniously in your ear along with world music, jazz, country music, rock in all its varieties, rap, pop, techno, post-rock, and more.

Classical Music

Classical music: just what is meant by that? The ordinary meaning of "classical" or "classic" is something old and established and valued on that account. The term is applied to many kinds of music, as we know: Classic Jazz, Classic Rock, even Classic Rap. "Classical music" itself can be very old indeed; it covers more than a thousand years of music as practiced and heard in Europe and America. You may also hear this music called "art music," or "Western music," or music of the Western tradition.

Classical music continues today; musical composition in the classical tradition is probably being taught this semester at your own college or university. The coverage in this book extends to music composed fifteen years ago by a composer who was then in her thirties. But nobody doubts that the great age of classical music is in the past. (Some would say the same for poetry, and even painting. Some would say the same for jazz . . .) Listening to classical music is listening to history. Why do that?

appraising hundreds of music Web sites for the Appendix and companion Web site, and to Tom Millioto, who reviewed every CD track timing in the text, and to Fletcher Moore and Professor Andrew Dell'Antonio for creating our newly enhanced electronic Listening Charts. Thanks are also due to the cartographers at Mapping Specialists Ltd.

The production of a major textbook is a complex, arduous process drawing on professionals from very many areas. This time around we had a terrific team consisting of some old friends, some new. We are indebted to Joan Feinberg of Bedford/St. Martin's for her enthusiastic support, Editor in Chief (Boston) Karen Henry for her wise and deft guidance, our superb text editor Maura Shea, equally superb production editor Karen Baart, and compositor and layout wizard DeNee Reiton Skipper, as well as art director Donna Dennison, new media editor David Mogolov, permissions editor Sandy Schechter, editorial assistant Anne Noyes, and production assistants Kristen Merrill and Michaela Dodd. Our oldest good friends are still with us: picture consultant Elaine Bernstein and Tom Laskey of Sony Special Products. (Tom is voted MVP, having made spectacular saves on the distinctly unlevel playing field known as the recording industry.) The high quality of *Listen* is a tribute to the expertise, dedication, and artistry of all these people, and we are indebted to them all.

Finally, warm thanks to Davitt Moroney for recording the Frescobaldi Suite for Unit II, on the seventeenth-century Spanish organ (in meantone tuning) by Greg Harrold at the University of California at Berkeley.

J. K.

G. T.

Berkeley and Philadelphia, 2003

/   The ***Test Bank*** (by Jane Viemeister) has 1,290 multiple-choice and 560 essay questions. It serves as a database for a Computerized Test-Generation System, available in a cross-platform CD-ROM, which makes it easy to tailor exams on your IBM-compatible or Macintosh computer. It is also available in a print version.

/   The ***Overhead Transparencies*** set includes acetates of each of the Listening Charts in this edition, with several other diagrams and texts and translations from the book.

/   ***Videos and DVDs of live performances*** of works discussed in this edition are available to qualified adopters. Contact your local Bedford/St. Martin's sales representative for more information.

/   ***E-content for Online Learning*** includes special content from *Listen* that helps instructors using the book develop custom Web sites with Web CT and Blackboard.

Ultimately, though, this text owes its success less to "features" than to two basic attributes, which we have been grateful to hear about many times from many instructors over the history of *Listen*. *Listen* is distinctive in its writing style and, related to that, in the sense it conveys of personal involvement with the music that is treated. The tone is lively and alert, authoritative but not stiff and not without humor. We sound (because we are) engaged with music and we work to engage the student. One should never condescend to students, any more than one should begrudge them careful explanation of matters that we as musicians find elementary.

     The excitement and joy that the experience of music can provide—this, more than historical or analytical data about music—is what most of us want to pass on to our students. This is what teaching is about (which is why CD-ROMs will never replace live instructors), and this is what we have always tried to do in *Listen*.

Acknowledgments

It remains to express the authors' gratitude to the numerous battle-scarred "music apprec" instructors who have reviewed sections of the book in draft and given us the benefit of their advice for this revision. Their criticisms and suggestions have significantly improved the text, as have the market surveys in which an even larger number of instructors have generously participated. In addition to the users of previous editions who over the years have given us suggestions, we wish to thank:

Mary Catherine Adams, James Madison University
James Arnwine, Pasadena City College
Joseph Baldassare, Boise State University
Mary Kay Bauer, Western Carolina University
Hubert Beckwith, George Mason University
Ian Bent, Columbia University
Steven Bresnen, Bucks County Community College
Geoffrey Burgess, SUNY Stony Brook
Angela Carlson, Oregon State University
Keith Clifton, University of Central Arkansas
Richard Cole, Virginia Polytechnic Institute and State College
Steven Cornelius, Bowling Green State University
Robert Culbertson, Lamar University
Vicki Curry, University of Utah
Andrew Dell'Antonio, University of Texas–Austin
Jeffrey Donovick, St. Petersburg College
Stuart Alan Duke, Truckee Meadows Community College
JanClaire Elliott, Pt. Loma Nazarene University
David Feingold, Western Washington University
Lawrence Ferrara, City College of San Francisco
Karen Garrison, Auburn University
Laura Greenberg, John Jay College–CUNY
Rolf Groesbeck, University of Arkansas–Little Rock
Michael Grose, University of Oregon
David Haas, University of Georgia
Kimberly Harris, Collin County Community College
Hillary Hight, Kenesaw State University
Jaren Hinckley, Brigham Young University
David Johansen, Southeastern Louisiana University
Randall Johnson, University of Guam
Folkert H. Kadyk, Pennsylvania State University–Delaware City
Jeffrey Kallberg, University of Pennsylvania
Maiko Kawabata, SUNY Stony Brook
Ken Keaton, Florida Atlantic University
Thomas Kittinger, Harrisburg Area Community College
Nancy Kudlawiec, University of West Alabama

Beth Anne Lee-De Amici, University of Virginia
Andrew Levin, Clemson University
Kay Lipton, Pasadena City College
Peggy Lupton, Cape Fear Community College
Melissa Mann, University of Connecticut–Storrs
Robert Mann, Stephen F. Austin State University
Ross Mann, Bucks County Community College
Karen Marston, San Jacinto College
David Maves, College of Charleston
Kevin McCarthy, University of Colorado–Boulder
Michael McGowan, Panola College
Herbert Midgley, Stephen F. Austin State University
Simon Morrison, Princeton University
Rena Mueller, New York University
Lynn Raley, Emory & Henry College
Jennifer Roth-Burnette, Birmingham-Southern College
George Ruckert, Massachusetts Institute of Technology
Kevin Salfen, University of North Texas
Michael Samball, Boise State University
Carolyn Sanders, University of Alabama–Huntsville
Jack Sheinbaum, University of Denver
William Shepherd, University of Northern Iowa
Marc Siegel, Cape Fear Community College
Glenn Stanley, University of Connecticut–Storrs
Michael Strasser, Baldwin-Wallace College
Helen Stringham, Salt Lake Community College
Jonathan Sturm, Iowa State University
Katherine Syer, University of Illinois–Urbana
Dane Teter, El Camino College
Richard Thorell, Indiana University of Pennsylvania
Christopher Ulffers, East Carolina University
Roger Walworth, Judson College
Scott Warfield, Centre College
Mary Joanna White, Cape Fear Community College
Noel Wilkins, San Jacinto College Central
Cathryn Wilkinson, Concordia University
Charles Youmans, Pennsylvania State University
Steve Zohn, Temple University

Professor Mark Harbold of Elmhurst College agreed to prepare the instructors' manual for *Listen,* Brief Fifth Edition, as he has done so successfully for previous editions. We are very grateful to him, to Dr. Jane Viemeister for writing hundreds of questions for the testbank and online listening and content quizzes, to Dr. Kristi Brown, who has done a fantastic job of searching and